A Bright
Future

Future
A Bright

Iris Howden

Published in association with
The Basic Skills Agency

Hodder & Stoughton

A MEMBER OF THE HODDER HEADLINE GROUP

Acknowledgements
Illustrations: Jim Eldridge.
Cover: Ruth Thomlevold/NB Illustration.

Orders: please contact Bookpoint Ltd, 130 Milton Park, Abingdon, Oxon OX14
4SB. Telephone: (44) 01235 827720, Fax: (44) 01235 400454. Lines are open from
9.00–6.00, Monday to Saturday, with a 24 hour message answering service.

British Library Cataloguing in Publication Data
A catalogue record for this title is available from The British Library

ISBN 0 340 86948 8

First published 1998
This edition published 2002
Impression number   10 9 8 7 6 5 4 3 2 1
Year   2007 2006 2005 2004 2003 2002

Typeset by Fakenham Photosetting Ltd, Fakenham, Norfolk.
Printed in Great Britain for Hodder & Stoughton Educational, a division of
Hodder Headline Plc, 338 Euston Road, London NW1 3BH by Athenaeum
Press Ltd, Gateshead, Tyne & Wear.

Contents

1
All Work and No Play

It was a long hot summer.
Every day I sat in my bedroom.
I shared it with my sister, Julie.
I was always working away at my books.

I would read my set texts,
make notes and write essays.
Even though it was stuffy,
I kept the windows shut.
That way I didn't hear
next door's dog barking.
Their children shouting or a radio playing.

'You should get out in the fresh air,'
my Mum told me. 'Get some sun.'
But if I went in the garden
I couldn't work.
Not with Grandad there, sitting in his chair.
He went on and on and on.
Telling me how things were better in his day.
How the weather was nicer.
The food had more taste,
the streets were cleaner.
He got on my nerves.

'Look at you,' he'd say.
'17 going on 18 and still at school.
You don't know you're born!
I'd been at work three years
by the time I was your age.
Down the pit at 14 I was.'

'Yes, Dad,' Mum told him.

'But things are different now.

You can't get anywhere without exams.

Anna's going to make something of her life.

She's going to university.

There's a bright future ahead of her.'

'Sitting around all day reading books,'

Grandad went on.

'Young people don't know

what hard work is.'

'Don't talk to me about hard work,'

my Mum said.

'I work hard enough to keep us all.'

That shut him up. It was true.

My Mum got up at five every day.

She was at work by six cleaning offices.

'I don't mind putting the hours in,'

she'd say.

'To give my girls a better chance in life.'

So I left Grandad alone.

Let Julie make his tea the way he liked it
– strong and sweet.

Let her fetch his paper from the shop.

Find his glasses, his matches,
the cigarettes that were so bad for him.

He had a weak chest and
they made him cough.

I could hear him all night.

Cough, cough, cough.

Julie was always his favourite.
She knew how to handle him.
How to get round him.
'You're a good girl, Julie,' he'd say.
'You look after your Grandad.
Our Anna thinks she's too good
to fetch and carry for an old man.'

2
The Fair

I knew Grandad thought I was stuck up.
Julie's friends thought so too.
They always had plenty to say.
'Are you going to go to the disco, Anna?
What are you wearing? Who's taking you?
How's your boyfriend, Greg?'

'No, I'm not going to the disco,' I'd say.
'I'm working. And Greg's not my boyfriend.'
I tried to take no notice of them.

I liked Greg. He was a good friend.
I tried not to listen when they called
him pizza face or four eyes.
He couldn't help having bad skin
or having to wear glasses.

He and I were in our last year at school.
Our school used to be quite run down.
Then we got a new Headmaster, Mr James.
He was brilliant. He had time for you.
Mr James made sure we stayed on
if we had any hope of passing our exams.
Greg and I were his star pupils.

We were doing the same subjects:
English, French and History.
So we spent a lot of time together.
Mr James took us for English sometimes.
He was a good teacher.
He made books come alive.

But it was hard work.
It took hours to do my homework.

I spent every spare minute reading.
Sometimes it all got too much.
So when Julie and her friends
talked about going to the fair
I agreed to go with them.

I needed a break.
After working so hard,
I wanted to have some fun.
The fair came every year, in September.
It was held on a field by the river.
It began on Friday and stayed for a week.
You could hear the music from our house.
I really wanted to go.

When we got there, Julie's gang
acted like little kids.
They were yelling and screaming.
Jumping on and off the rides.
I felt a bit of a fool, left alone,
going round on a painted horse.
Driving a dodgem car on my own.

One of the lads who worked on the fair
came to collect the money.
He sat down next to me.
'All on your own?' he asked.
'Mind if I keep you company?'
He put a strong brown arm round me.
There was a tattoo on it.
A bird. A swallow, I think it was.

He was very good looking.
Tall, with long hair tied back
and deep blue eyes.

He had a lovely voice, a soft Irish accent.
He told me his name was Billy.
Then he asked me mine.
'Anna.' – The way he said it
sent shivers down my spine.

He asked me to meet him the next day.
We walked by the river before the fair began.
After that, I began to sneak out,
late at night, to meet him.
In the darkness Billy held me tight.
He kissed me and called me darling
in his soft Irish voice.
I had never met anyone like him.

I had never been with a boy before.
Billy made me feel special.
I could not say 'no' to him.
We had a week of secret meetings.
A week of stolen kisses.
A week of loving one another.
Then the fair packed up and left.
I never saw him again.

3
A Shock

_____

The weeks passed.

I worked hard at school.

I wrote more essays and got good grades.

Greg and I began to apply to universities.

He put down for the same ones as me.

I went on interview and did quite well.

I knew that I would get a place

if I got the right grades.

Then it all went wrong.
I began to feel sick in the morning.
At first I thought I had a stomach bug.
Then it dawned on me what was wrong.
I had missed two periods.
I must be pregnant!

I didn't know what to do.
So I did nothing.
Maybe I thought it would just go away.
I didn't even tell Julie.
She'd be bound to tell Mum.
I carried on as though nothing
was the matter.

Then I began to put on weight.
Not much at first, but by Christmas
I looked quite plump.
I took to wearing big baggy jumpers
to hide the bulge.
Soon my skirt wouldn't do up.
It was only a matter of time
before Mum spotted it.

Things came to a head on Christmas Day.
A time when families always seem to fall out.
You start off full of the Christmas spirit
and end up at each others' throats.
I had a row with Julie.
It was about something and nothing.
She ended up calling me a fat cow.
Mum told her off but I saw her looking
at me in an odd way.

She had seen my bulky body.
Heard me throwing up in the morning.
Mum soon put two and two together.
The next few days were dreadful.

At first Mum wouldn't speak to me.
Then she wanted to know details.
How and when and most of all who.
'Who is the father?' she shouted.
'Is it that stupid Greg?
Just wait till I get my hands on him.'
I tried to calm her down.

By now Julie knew. She and her friends
looked at me with new eyes.
Anna the swot had got herself in trouble.
She wasn't so clever after all.
My ears burned.
I knew they were talking about me.

Grandad of course was the worst.
'It's a disgrace,' he shouted.
'The girl's nothing but a slut!
She should be thrown out of the house.
We waited till we were wed in my day.'
'Yes, Dad,' Mum said. 'Give it a rest.
Going on like that won't help matters.'

Mum was great. She stood by me.
By this time it was too late to have
an abortion even if I wanted one.
'This baby's family,' Mum told me.
'We'll manage somehow.'
She came with me to see Mr James.
He was shocked but he tried not
to show it.

'We must make the best of things,' he told us.
'Anna can carry on at school till Easter.
After that she can work at home.
She must take her A levels
after all the work she's put in.'

Then my Mum broke down and cried.
Right there. In front of the Headmaster.
I had never seen her cry before.
Not even when my Dad died.

I should have felt embarrassed.
But I didn't.
I just felt very sorry for her.
Sorry for all the pain I'd caused her.

4

My Baby is Born

My baby was born in exam week.
I had only taken two papers,
and I had made a hash of them.
The weather was hot. I felt ill.
I was so big by now.
I was dragging myself about.
The baby was not due for
another two weeks
when I started having pains.
My Mum rang for a taxi.
We went to the hospital.

I was lucky. It was quite an easy birth.
The baby was a boy.
As soon as I saw him I knew
that I could never give him up.
I was going to keep him.
I called him Joshua Charles.
The Charles was after my dad.
That pleased my mum.
I don't know why I chose the name Joshua.
I just liked it.
He would be called Josh for short.

In the hospital I felt sad.
All the other babies had proud fathers
to come and see them.
Josh would never know his dad.
Even though I loved my baby,
I knew it would not be easy bringing him up.
I had been stupid, taking risks.
Getting pregnant so young.
Now I would have to live with it.

Mr James came to see me.
He brought a pile of books.
'You can study at home,' he said.
'Re-sit your exams in November.'
But I knew I wouldn't do that.
Baby Josh would take up all my time.

Greg came as well.
He brought a teddy bear for Josh.
He was going to university.
'I don't have to go,' he said.
'I could stay here. Look after you.
Get a job. We could get married.'

'Don't be daft,' I told him.
'Going to university is all you ever wanted.
But keep in touch. Write to me.
Let me know how things go.'
I was very touched by his offer.
But I could never marry Greg.
I did not love him.
It would not be right to tie him down.

We went home. It was awful.
I had no idea how to look after a baby.
No idea how much time they took up.
How much gear they needed.
'Can you move some of this stuff?'
Grandad would say. 'I want to sit down.
Can't you stop that baby crying?
I can't get a wink of sleep.'

The night times were the worst.
Josh needed feeding so often.
I was worn out.
I couldn't ask Mum to help at night.
She had to get up early for work.

Julie was tired too.
Josh kept her awake.
The room was very small.
We kept banging into the cot.
'It's no good,' I told Mum.
'I'll have to get my own place.
I'll go down to the council tomorrow.'

I was lucky.
In a matter of weeks
they were able to offer me a flat.
It was a bit scruffy but it wasn't damp.
And it was in quite a nice area.
'It'll do,' Mum said.
'When we've given it
a good clean and a lick of paint.'

She was so good about everything.
She helped me get some furniture.
She paid for the move.
She looked after Josh while
I painted the walls.

When it was done I looked round
my sitting room.
I held Josh in my arms.
'What do you think of your new home?'
I asked him. We were on our own.

5

On Our Own

That first winter was hard for me.
I had to learn how to cook and clean.
How to look after Josh.
Money was tight.
I could just about manage on benefit
but there were no treats.
I could not afford clothes or a night out.

Not that I had a baby sitter.
My Mum had her hands full with Grandad.
His chest was worse in the winter.

If I asked Julie to baby sit
she brought all her mates round.
I came back once to find Josh crying.
They didn't hear him above the noise
of the CDs they were playing.
So I stopped asking her.

I made friends with other single mums.
Layla, a Pakistani girl.
Susie, who was only sixteen.
Karen, who had twins one year old.
It was good to have some company.

One day was really bad.
Josh had a cold.
He wouldn't sleep.
The weather was bad.
My only pair of shoes let in the rain.
I felt very bad.
I sat by the fire
and read the free newspaper.
It came through the door every week.

I looked through the adverts
for second hand things.
Josh could do with a play pen.
He was crawling now.
Into everything.
He kept trying to put his fingers
into plug sockets.
I had to watch him all the time.

Then I read the letters page.
One of the letters made me really angry.
It was about single mothers.

'Why do these girls think they have
a right to hand-outs?' the writer asked.
'I've seen them, smoking cigarettes,
dressed in the latest fashions.
All paid for by us tax-payers.'

It made my blood boil.
I was so mad I took a pad and pen
and began to write a reply.
Smoking cigarettes!
I could just about afford to eat.
I put down how I lived on beans
on toast or egg and chips.
I couldn't afford meat.

Dressed in the latest fashion!
I would have to search the charity
shops for another pair of shoes.

Once I started there was no stopping me.
I wrote about Layla being disowned
by her family when she had a baby.
I wrote about Susie, who couldn't get benefit
at first because she was under 18.
I wrote about Karen, who went without food
to heat the flat for her babies.

I wrote page after page.
Before I could change my mind
I went out and posted it.

A week later the editor rang me.
'We were very taken with your letter,' he said.
'We'd like to publish it as an article.
There'll be a fee of course.'
He asked me if I had any other ideas.
'We want to put the young person's
point of view,' he said.

So I began to work for him part-time.
He sent me out to talk to young people
in the area.
I went to schools and youth clubs.

I made a visit to the local college.
There were so many classes on offer.
There was even a crêche
where I could leave baby Josh.
I put my name down for word processing.
I'd need to know how to type
if I was going to be a writer.

A letter came from Greg.
It was full of news about his classes.
The clubs he'd joined at university.
The new friends he'd made.
I was full of envy but it gave me the push
I needed. It was time I started to study again.
I made up my mind to re-take my A levels.
It might take years but I'd get to university.
Then I'd be able to give Josh a better life.
He'd be proud of his mum.

I was thinking about this as I pushed
Josh's pram through the streets.
He'd run out of nappies.
We'd been to get some from the supermarket.
It was getting dark.
I didn't like going out at this time.
There was a gang of youths who hung
about on the corner at night.

One of them had a dog.
It was a big Alsatian. I was scared of it.
Afraid it might snap at Josh.

The boys were blocking the pavement.
I pushed the pram into the road.
They came towards me.
'Where are you off to darling?'
one of them said.
The dog began to bark.
It leapt towards me, pulling on its lead.
I stood still, afraid that if I moved
it would attack me.

Then a motor bike stopped at the kerb.
A young man in black leathers
pushed the visor of his helmet back.

'What's going on boys?' he asked.
'Nothing,' one of them said.
'We're just messing about.
Having a laugh. We're going now.'
They went away,
dragging the dog after them.

'Are you OK?' the motor cyclist asked.
'Yes, thanks,' I said.
'I hate that dog.
I'm always afraid he'll hurt my baby.'
'I'll walk with you,' he said.
'Make sure you get home safely.'

As he pushed his bike along he told me
his name was Steve.
He seemed really nice.
When he left me at the door of my flat
I hoped I would meet him again.

6
A New Start

In the new year I went to the college
to enrol for an English class.
It was on in the day time.
Josh could go to the crêche.
I filled in the forms and paid my fees.
I was just leaving when I bumped
into Steve.

'Hello,' he said, 'What are you doing here?'
I told him about the class I had joined.

'That's the same day as my maths class,'
he said. 'Do you fancy a coffee?'
He helped me get the buggy down the steps.

Over coffee he told me all about himself.
'I messed around at school,' he said.
'I left without taking exams.
Now I'm keen on electronics.
I'm working nights in a factory
that makes computers.
I'm only doing low level stuff as yet.
But there's a chance to get on
if I take exams. How about you?'

I told him all about myself.
How I'd failed my A levels.
How I was on my own with Josh.
He seemed to think I'd coped well.
I was pleased when he said Josh
was a credit to me.

I told Steve about my part time job.
How I was learning to type.
'I could get you a cheap word processor,'
he said.
'We often take old ones in part exchange.'
'Really?' I was thrilled.
My mum had given me
some money for Christmas.
'I'll see what I can do,' Steve said.

A few days later he brought one round.
He set it up for me on the table.
'This is great,' I said. 'Thanks a lot.'

After that Steve came round quite often.
He helped me do odd jobs in the flat.
Steve was good with Josh.
Josh loved it when Steve played with him.
Let him ride on his back.

Josh was coming up to a year old.
I wanted to give him a birthday party.
I asked my family and my friends:
Layla, Sue and Karen and their children.
I didn't know whether to ask Steve or not.
'I'm not sure it's your scene,' I told him.
'Come if you've nothing better to do.'

On the day I was up early.
I iced the cake.
Made some sandwiches.
I hung balloons around the room.
Josh had lots of cards.
I showed them to him before I put them up.
I wanted everything to be right.

I did not expect Steve to come.
But he did.
He brought a present for Josh.
He played with the children.
Talked to my friends.
Helped to amuse Grandad.
He even did the washing up.

My friends thought Steve was good looking.
'He's alright,' Karen said.
'It's not like that,' I told her.
'We're just good friends.'

My family liked him too.
Even Grandad called him 'A great bloke.'
'Steve seems very nice,' my Mum said.
But her look said 'Be careful.'

'It's OK,' I told her.
'I'm not going
to rush into anything.'
I had made one mistake.
I wasn't going to make another.

It was early days.
Maybe Steve and I would get together.
We'd have to wait and see.
I wanted someone pretty special
to be a dad for Josh.

I looked at my baby son,
lying asleep on Mum's sofa.
His thumb in his mouth.
One chubby arm around his teddy bear.

At that moment I had no regrets.
I did not care about the failed exams.
The missed chances.

My aim was to put things right.
Make up for lost time.
I would work hard to make sure
that Josh had a bright future too.